Let's Do Chores

Practicing the CH Sound

Ethan Lewis

Rosen
PHONICS
READERS

Rosen
Classroom™

Today is chore day.
We have many chores to do!

Mom lets me choose my chores.

I check on the chickens.
The chickens look good.

This chicken's name is Charlie!
Charlie is the best chicken.

I pick cherries
from our cherry tree.
I love cherries!

I cut cheese for lunch.

I chop food into chunks.

I wash the chairs.
The chairs were dirty!

I hang chimes in a tree.
The chimes make music.

The chores are all done!
Chores can be fun.

We did a good job with chores.
Mom gives us
chocolate cupcakes!

Writing Activity

- Using their fingers, ask students to trace the shape of the letter combination *ch* on this page.
- Ask students to trace the letter combination *ch* in the air.
- Using water or finger paint, ask students to write the letter combination *ch* on paper.

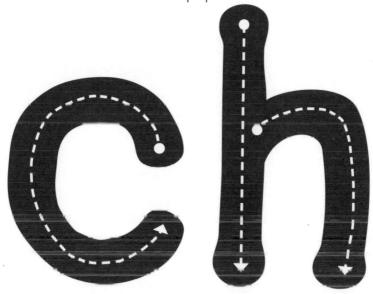

Word Count: 94

Published in 2017 by The Rosen Publishing Group, Inc.
29 East 21st Street, New York, NY 10010

Book Design: Jennifer Ryder-Talbot
Editor: Caitie McAneney

Photo Credits: Cover Billion Photos/Shutterstock.com; p. 2 Africa Studio/ Shutterstock.com; p. 3 Yuganov Konstantin/Shutterstock.com; p. 4 Thomas Zobl/ Shutterstock.com; p. 5 schankz/Shutterstock.com; p. 6 sakkmesterke/Shutterstock.com; p. 7 dogboxstudio/Shutterstock.com; p. 8 Krzysztof Slusarczyk/Shutterstock.com; p. 9 Freedom_Studio/Shutterstock.com; p. 10 tose/Shutterstock.com; p. 11 gorillaimages/ Shutterstock.com; p. 12 istetiana/Shutterstock.com.

ISBN: 9781508132349
6-pack ISBN: 9781508132356

Manufactured in the United States of America

CPSIA Compliance Information: Batch #WW17RC: For Further Information contact Rosen Publishing, New York, New York at 1-800-237-9932

Rosen
PHONICS
READERS

Rosen
Classroom

9 781508 132349

ISBN: 9781508132349
6-pack ISBN: 9781508132356

Max Packs a Box

Practicing the KS Sound

Whitney Walker

Rosen Phonics Readers
Max Packs a Box: Practicing the KS Sound

Instructional Guide

Word List

books	packs
box	rocks
clocks	snacks
forks	socks
fox	trucks
looks	walks
Max	

Teacher Talk

- Page through the book and point to each word that includes the letter combination *ks* or the letter *x*. Explain that each of these words includes the /ks/ sound. This is the sound made by the letter combination *ks* or the letter *x* in the words *packs*, *box*, and *socks*.

Group Activity

- Point to each word and its corresponding picture and say each word slowly. Ask students to listen for the /ks/ sound as you say the words.
- Say the words again, emphasizing the /ks/ sound. Ask students to point to the letter or letter combination that makes that sound. Does it appear at the beginning of the word, in the middle, or at the end?
- List the words and have students underline the *ks* or *x* in each word as you read it.

Extended Activity

- On a whiteboard or large sheet of paper, write incomplete words such as: si__, fi__, and bloc__. Have students complete the words by writing in the missing letter combination *ks* or the letter *x*. Ask students to decode the completed words and use them in sentences.